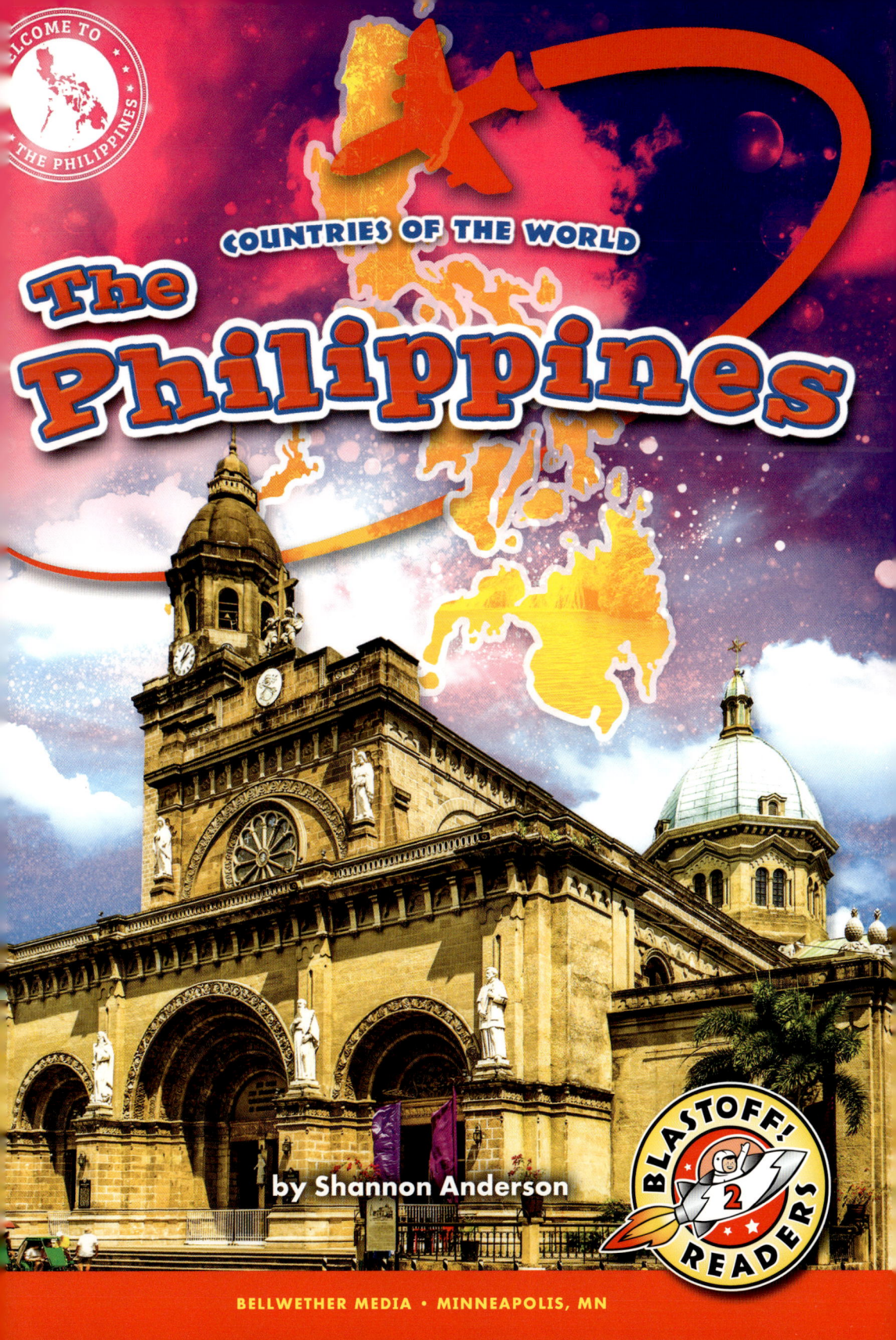

COUNTRIES OF THE WORLD

# The Philippines

by Shannon Anderson

BELLWETHER MEDIA • MINNEAPOLIS, MN

**Blastoff! Readers** are carefully developed by literacy experts to build reading stamina and move students toward fluency by combining standards-based content with developmentally appropriate text.

## LEVELS

**Level 1** provides the most support through repetition of high-frequency words, light text, predictable sentence patterns, and strong visual support.

**Level 2** offers early readers a bit more challenge through varied sentences, increased text load, and text-supportive special features.

**Level 3** advances early-fluent readers toward fluency through increased text load, less reliance on photos, advancing concepts, longer sentences, and more complex special features.

★ **Blastoff! Universe**

Reading Level

Grade K

Grades 1–3

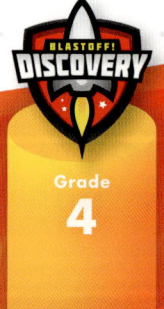
Grade 4

This edition first published in 2025 by Bellwether Media, Inc.

No part of this publication may be reproduced in whole or in part without written permission of the publisher. For information regarding permission, write to Bellwether Media, Inc., Attention: Permissions Department, 6012 Blue Circle Drive, Minnetonka, MN 55343.

Library of Congress Cataloging-in-Publication Data

LC record for The Philippines available at: https://lccn.loc.gov/2024012105

Text copyright © 2025 by Bellwether Media, Inc. BLASTOFF! READERS and associated logos are trademarks and/or registered trademarks of Bellwether Media, Inc. Bellwether Media is a division of Chrysalis Education Group.

Editor: Suzane Nguyen   Designer: Laura Sowers

Printed in the United States of America, North Mankato, MN.

# Table of Contents

| | |
|---|---|
| All About the Philippines | 4 |
| Land and Animals | 6 |
| Life in the Philippines | 12 |
| Philippines Facts | 20 |
| Glossary | 22 |
| To Learn More | 23 |
| Index | 24 |

# All About the Philippines

Manila

The Philippines is an island country in Asia. It has over 7,000 islands!

It sits in the Pacific Ocean. The capital is Manila.

# Land and Animals

The country is in the **Ring of Fire**. There are many mountains and **volcanoes**. Some of the volcanoes are still active!

Many lakes lie between the mountains.

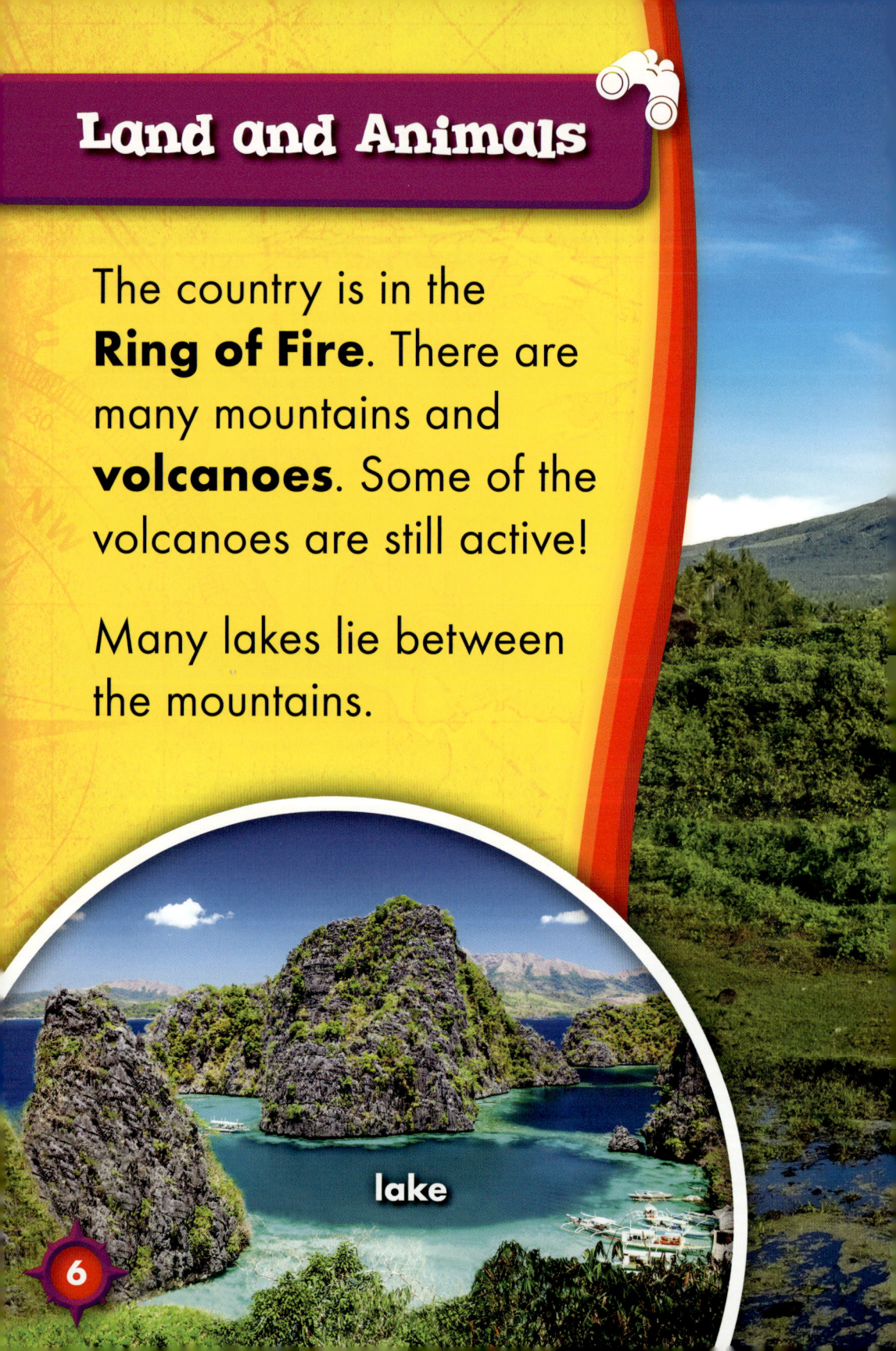

lake

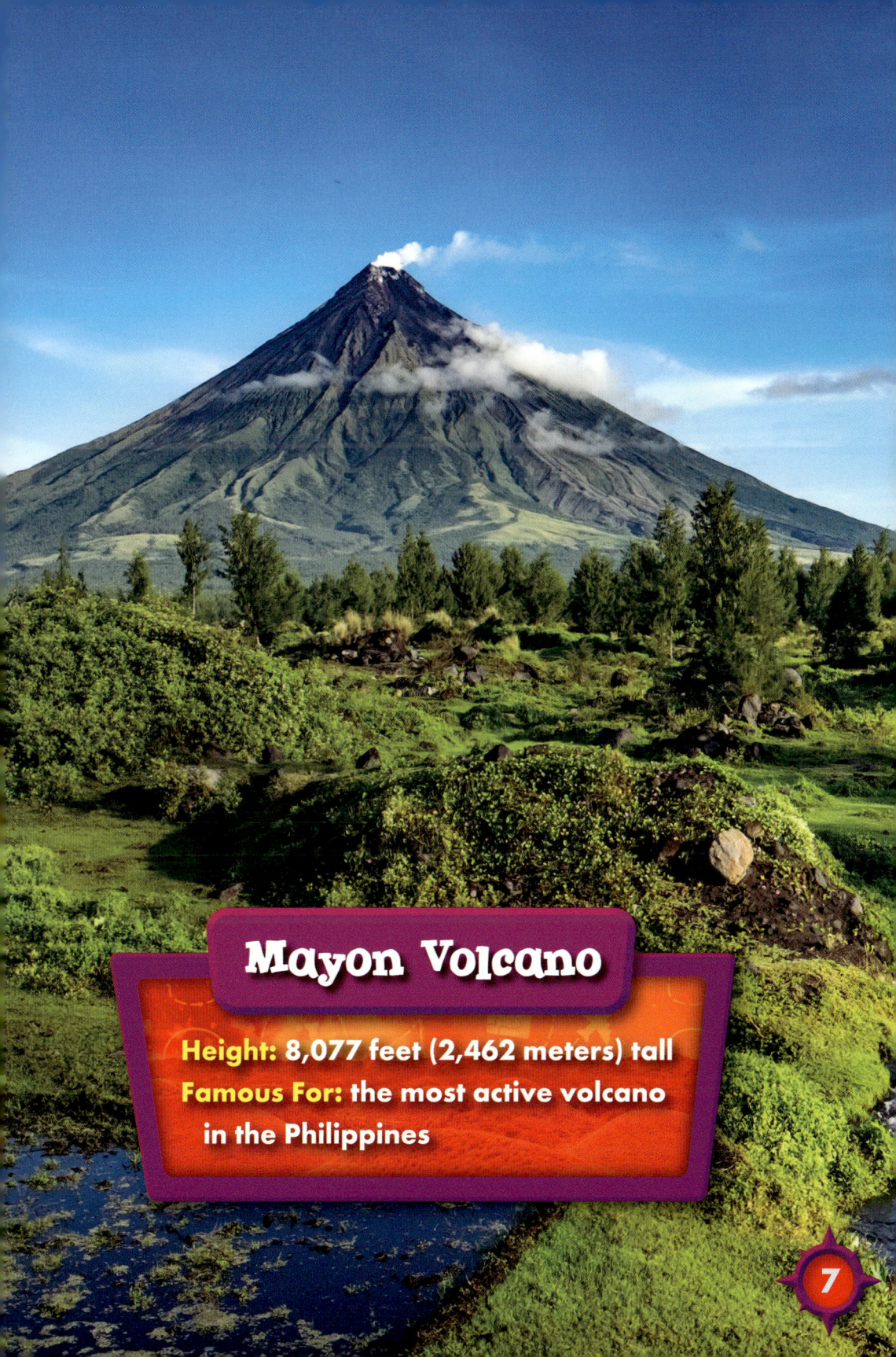

## Mayon Volcano

**Height:** 8,077 feet (2,462 meters) tall
**Famous For:** the most active volcano in the Philippines

The Philippines is a **tropical** country. The dry season is cooler.

The wet season has a lot of rain. **Monsoons** are common.

monsoon

Sea turtles swim in the ocean. Pangolins snap up **insects**.

leatherback turtle

# Animals of the Philippines

leatherback turtle

Philippine pangolin

Philippine flying lemur

Philippine eagle

Flying lemurs sail between trees. Philippine eagles hunt in forests.

# Life in the Philippines

Filipinos come from many **backgrounds**. Filipino is the main language. Tagalog is a common form. People also speak English.

Most Filipinos are **Roman Catholic**.

Roman Catholic church

martial art

basketball

Basketball is a favorite sport. Many people enjoy **martial arts**.

People like water sports, too. Windsurfing and diving are popular. Family time is also important.

windsurfing

Rice is a **staple** food.
It is eaten with meals.
*Balut* is a duck egg dish.

### Filipino Foods

rice

balut

milkfish

adobo

milkfish

Milkfish is a common seafood. *Adobo* is seasoned pork or chicken.

Christmas is a big holiday. Some people **celebrate** Christmas for months!

Easter is big, too. Churches hold a special service. Filipinos love to gather with their families.

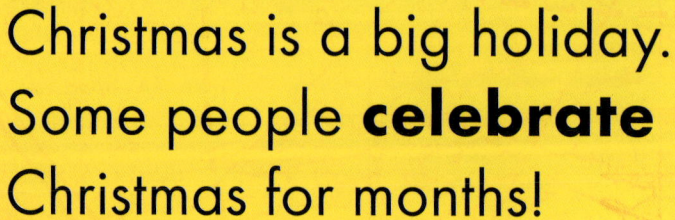
Easter

Christmas

# Philippines Facts

**Size:**
115,831 square miles (300,000 square kilometers)

**Population:**
116,434,200 (2023)

**National Holiday:**
Independence Day (June 12)

**Main Language:**
Filipino

**Capital City:**
Manila

## Famous Face

**Name:** Lea Salonga

**Famous For:** singer and actress known for singing in the Disney movies *Aladdin* and *Mulan*

# Religions

- other 15%
- Muslim 6%
- Roman Catholic 79%

# Top Landmarks

**Banaue Rice Terraces**

**Chocolate Hills**

**San Agustin Church**

# Glossary

**backgrounds**—people's experiences, knowledge, and family histories

**celebrate**—to do something special or fun for an event, occasion, or holiday

**insects**—small animals with six legs and bodies divided into three parts

**martial arts**—different sports or skills that first started as ways to fight or stay safe

**monsoons**—winds that change direction each season; monsoons bring heavy rain.

**Ring of Fire**—an area along the edge of the Pacific Ocean characterized by active volcanoes and frequent earthquakes

**Roman Catholic**—people belonging or relating to the Christian church that is led by the pope

**staple**—a widely used food or other item

**tropical**—having to do with a place that is hot and wet

**volcanoes**—holes in the earth; when a volcano erupts, hot ash, gas, or melted rock called lava shoots out.

# To Learn More

### AT THE LIBRARY

Grack, Rachel. *Pangolins*. Minneapolis, Minn.: Bellwether Media, 2025.

Mattern, Joanne. *Philippines*. Minneapolis, Minn.: Jump!, 2019.

Romulo, Liana. *Filipino Children's Favorite Stories: Fables, Myths and Fairy Tales.* Tuttle Publishing, 2019.

### ON THE WEB

# FACTSURFER

Factsurfer.com gives you a safe, fun way to find more information.

1. Go to www.factsurfer.com.
2. Enter "the Philippines" into the search box and click 🔍.
3. Select your book cover to see a list of related content.

# Index

animals, 10, 11
Asia, 4
basketball, 14
capital (see Manila)
Christmas, 18, 19
diving, 15
Easter, 18
English, 12
family, 15, 18
Filipino, 12, 13
food, 16, 17
forests, 11
island, 4
lakes, 6
Manila, 4, 5
map, 5
martial arts, 14
Mayon Volcano, 7
monsoons, 9

mountains, 6
Pacific Ocean, 5, 10
people, 12, 14, 15, 18
Philippines facts, 20–21
rain, 9
Ring of Fire, 6
Roman Catholic, 12
say hello, 13
Tagalog, 12
volcanoes, 6, 7
windsurfing, 15

The images in this book are reproduced through the courtesy of: Richie Chan, front cover, p. 21 (San Agustin Church); Mini Onion, p. 3; Aleksandr Medvedkov, pp. 4-5; saiko3p, p. 6; Puripat Lertpunyaroj, pp. 6-7; Simon Dannhauer, pp. 8-9; CherylRamalho, p. 9; Rawlinson_Photography, pp. 10-11; wildestanimal, p. 11 (leatherback turtle); Shukran888, p. 11 (Philippine pangolin); blickwinkel/ Alamy, p. 11 (Philippine flying lemur); Keeriwala Gamage Dilshan Sanjeewa Gamage, p. 11 (Philippine eagle); Tang Yan Song, p. 12; jejim, pp. 12-13; Neil Bussey, pp. 14-15 (market art); SujanGurang, p. 14 (basketball); Iuliia Shcherbakova, p. 15 (windsurfing); Doraiplopez, p. 16 (rice); Logunov Maxim, p. 16 (*balut*); sockagphoto, p. 16 (milkfish); Brent Hofacker, p. 16 (*adobo*); Art Phaneuf/ Alamy, p. 17; SOPA Images Limited/ Alamy, p. 18; :fazon1, pp. 18-19; Millenius, p. 20 (flag); MediaPunch Inc/ Alamy, p. 20 (Lea Salonga); Frolova_Elena, p. 21 (Banaue Rice Terraces); Pelikh Alexey, p. 21 (Chocolate Hills); Edwin Verin, p. 22.